DATING VIOLENCE

LAURA LA BELLA

ROSEN
PUBLISHING®

New York

Published in 2016 by The Rosen Publishing Group, Inc.
29 East 21st Street, New York, NY 10010

Library of Congress Cataloging in Publication Data

La Bella, Laura.
Dating violence/Laura La Bella.—First edition.
       pages cm.—(Confronting violence against women)
Includes bibliographical references and index.
ISBN 978-1-4994-6030-8 (library bound)—ISBN 978-1-4994-6031-5 (pbk.)—
ISBN 978-1-4994-6032-2 (6-pack)
1. Dating violence—Juvenile literature. I. Title.
HQ801.83.L32 2015
362.88—dc23

                                                              2014045491

Manufactured in the United States of America

CONTENTS

INTRODUCTION

In March 2014, Ray Rice, a National Football League (NFL) running back with the Baltimore Ravens, got into an argument with Janay Palmer, his then fiancée, in a hotel elevator. As the disagreement escalated, Rice punched Palmer in the face, knocking her out. Initially, NFL commissioner Roger Goodell gave Rice a two-game ban, which would have prevented him from playing the first two games of the 2014 season. That July, Rice released a statement saying his actions were inexcusable and that he and Palmer, who married Rice just weeks after the incident, were in counseling together.

It wasn't until months later, when videotape from a surveillance camera *inside* the elevator became public, that any meaningful action was taken against Rice. The tape revealed that not only did Rice punch Palmer in the face, but he also dragged her unconscious body into the hallway of the hotel when the elevator doors opened. When the NFL and the Ravens reviewed the video, Rice was let go from the team, and the NFL suspended him indefinitely.

Rice's assault on his fiancée is just one example of the kind of violence that can take place in a relationship between two people who are dating. Dating violence is a prevalent problem, and teens are not immune. In a nationwide survey conducted in 2011 by the Centers for Disease Control and Prevention, 9.4 percent of high

Ray Rice, a running back for the National Football League's Baltimore Ravens, attends an appeals hearing with his wife, Janay Palmer, whom he is accused of beating.

school students reported having been hit, slapped, or physically hurt on purpose by their boyfriend or girlfriend. The survey also revealed that one in three students reported some form of abuse and that two out of three never reported the abuse to an adult.

As a teenager, it can sometimes be difficult to ascertain what constitutes abusive or violent behavior in a relationship. Playful teasing can quickly become hurtful when the comments become emotionally painful. Your partner's constant wondering where and with whom you are may seem like innocent curiosity. But when the questions lead to erratic and controlling behavior—your partner becomes angry with you for talking to friends or tries to control where you go or what you wear—you may find yourself in a potentially troubled relationship. Understanding what dating violence is can help you recognize when you are in a potentially violent relationship or help you avoid getting involved with someone who could become violent.

Furthermore, erroneous reports, such as the article titled "A Rape on Campus" that was featured in the December 2014 issue of Rolling Stone, further cloud the issue. Rapes on college campuses (and in lower-level schools) do indeed happen, but as revealed by the Columbia Journalism Review, this particular story got it wrong, most unfortunately casting doubt on an all-too real and underreported occurrence in the teen years and beyond.

Such suspicions and circumstances notwithstanding, if you do find yourself in a violent relationship, there are many local and national resources available for you to get the help you need. These organizations can assist you in understanding the causes of dating violence and the impact of certain behaviors. They can also provide intervention to help you manage the violent behavior you are experiencing until you can safely end the relationship, give you information about resources available to you, and offer support and information on healing from the effects of dating violence. You can also turn to these organizations for guidance on how to help and support a friend who is in a violent relationship, as well as provide support if you find that you are the one experiencing feelings of anger or possessiveness toward your partner.

CHAPTER 1

What Is Dating Violence?

Kristen Rambler's high school boyfriend Keith lavished her with flowers and repeatedly told her how much he loved her. But it wasn't until he shoved her, in front of friends at a graduation party in North Huntington, Pennsylvania, that she first saw signs that he might be violent. That summer the abuse continued. In one incident, when Kristen accidently spilled furniture polish on his carpet, Keith grabbed her by her hair, dragged her to the carpet, and slammed her head against the floor and the metal bunk beds.

That fall they both left for different colleges, but the abuse continued for more than a year, with Kristen often blaming herself for Keith's behavior. The following Valentine's Day, Keith beat Kristen when she made a surprise visit to his college to celebrate the holiday. This time, local authorities were called, and Keith was arrested. But Kristen declined to press charges. She found herself lying about her bruises to her friends and hiding the news from her family that she and he were still a couple. The summer after their freshman year of college, Kristen knew she had to break off the relationship for good. She called Keith and told him it was over.

The next day, as Kristen was getting ready to spend the day with a friend, Keith showed up at her parents' house with a gun. Keith shot a male friend of Kristen's who had arrived to pick her up for the day, and after holding Kristen at gunpoint, he turned the gun on himself and committed suicide. Kristen later found an e-mail Keith had sent her before he arrived at her house. It said he was going to kill himself to prove he loved her. Since his death, Kristen has been attending professional counseling to help her cope with the aftereffects of the physical and emotional abuse she experienced.

Dating violence is a pattern of fear and abuse that occurs between two people who are involved in an intimate relationship.

When Optimism Meets Reality

Kristen's story is similar to those of so many young women who find themselves in violent relationships. "I loved him and I didn't want to leave him. He was my first love," she told ABC News's *Good Morning America* in an interview. "You keep thinking this person's going to change, but they're not."

Dating violence, which is sometimes called relationship abuse, intimate partner violence, relationship violence, or dating abuse, is defined as a pattern of abusive behavior that occurs over a course of time and is used to exert power and control over one person by another. The majority of the time it happens between couples who are currently dating or have dated in the past. It can happen when couples are physically together, while on a date or hanging out, or it can occur electronically via social media, texting, or e-mail.

The behaviors used can encompass a wide range of controlling and/or violent acts, including physical, emotional, verbal, psychological, and sexual abuse. An abuser often has intense feelings of jealousy; commits acts of coercion, manipulation, or possessiveness; and exhibits violent, threatening behavior. Dating violence tends to increase in severity the longer a couple is together.

Types of Violent and Threatening Behaviors

You may experience several types of violent and threatening behaviors during a relationship. It's important to remember that none of them is acceptable or any part of a healthy relationship.

Controlling Behaviors

Controlling behaviors, such as telling you what to wear, with whom you can hang out, or where you can go, are actions your partner does to manipulate you into doing what he (or, less frequently, she) want you to do. Your partner may make you feel guilty for not following his or her directions; become angry at you for hanging out with your friends; call or text you frequently to find out where you are, with whom, and what you're doing; influence what you should wear and how you should act; tell you who you can and can't befriend; or act as though he or she has to be with you all the time, no matter what you're doing.

Verbal and Emotional Abuse

Verbal and emotional abuse are nonphysical behaviors, such as threats, insults, humiliation, intimidation, stalking, harassment, and isolation. These words and behaviors can begin to negatively affect your self-esteem. You may begin to feel worthless, threatened, and less confident about yourself or your abilities. Verbal and emotional abuse is a way for your partner to get you to become more dependent on him or her, giving him or her more control over your life. Emotional abuse can become so harmful that you can begin to believe the things your partner tells you.

Physical Abuse

If your partner uses physical force, such as shoving, punching, slapping, pinching, hitting, kicking, pulling your hair, squeezing any part of you so hard that it hurts, or strangling you, you are being physically abused. Physical abuse can also include the times when your partner grabs your face to make you look at him or her, pulling on your clothing to keep you from walking away, and throwing objects at or near you.

Sexual Abuse

Sexual abuse is when your partner forces you to do something sexual that you do not want to do, restricts your access to birth control or condoms, ignores your refusal to engage in sexual activities, or

Dating violence involves a range of violent and threatening behavior, from physical and sexual abuse to digital assault and emotional abuse.

repeatedly pressures you to perform sexual acts you don't want to perform. Some examples of sexual abuse are unwanted kissing or touching, rape or attempted rape, or sexual contact when your decision-making ability is impaired from alcohol or drugs. Even if you are dating, it's still considered rape if your partner forces you to have sex despite your repeated attempts to say no.

Digital Abuse

The technology age has increased our ability to communicate with one another. It has also provided a new avenue for abuse. Digital

HOW TO RECOGNIZE AN UNHEALTHY RELATIONSHIP

There are significant differences between healthy and unhealthy relationships. In general, a healthy relationship should make you feel good about yourself. You should feel supported by your partner and have some degree of happiness or contentment. If you don't, you may be engaged in an unhealthy relationship. What follows are examples of behaviors and attitudes that can help you recognize if you are engaged in an unhealthy or potentially violent relationship:

- *Giving freely vs. giving to get.* When you genuinely care for another person, you give your support and compassion without the expectation of something in return. In an unhealthy relationship, your abuser may lend support, but in exchange you may be expected to give up something.
- *Knowing each other vs. changing each other.* In a caring relationship, partners are free to be who they are without fear of criticism. In an unhealthy relationship, your partner may try to change who you are or want you to conform to what he or she wants you to be.
- *Privacy vs. exposure.* In healthy relationships, you and your partner protect the time you have together and encourage each other to be better people. You don't share each other's secrets or intimate experiences with other people. In an unhealthy relationship, one partner

Not all abuse is physical. An unhealthy relationship can include many types of abuse, including making you feel scared, insecure, ignored, or guilty.

may use the other's insecurities or private relations as weapons against the other. One's weaknesses become the focus of jokes by the other, and private details of your life together, such as kissing or other intimate acts, may be used to embarrass you. Abusers often expose information about their partners online.

- **Repair vs. revenge.** Arguments are a normal and healthy part of a relationship. But how you fight with your partner and how you resolve disagreements are different in healthy and unhealthy relationships. In healthy relationships, partners listen to the other's

(continued on the next page)

(continued from the previous page)

words, appreciate feelings expressed, and seek ways to positively remedy problems together. In unhealthy relationships, fights can be vindictive. You or your partner may use the argument as an opportunity to blame, hurt, or reject the other person.

- *Shared goals vs. selfishness.* When you truly care for another person, you encourage the other's goals, hopes, and dreams. You want to see the other person do well and be happy. In an unhealthy relationship, one partner may seek to make his or her goals the main focus, may discourage the other from pursuing an interest, or make it difficult for the partner to follow a passion or dream.

abuse is when your partner uses texting or social media (Twitter, Facebook, Instagram, etc.) to bully, harass, stalk, intimidate, or embarrass you. Posting information about you or sharing intimate photos or videos is digital abuse.

Warning Signs

Knowing and understanding the warning signs of dating violence can help you recognize if you are engaged in an unhealthy relationship. The most common warning signs of dating violence are when your partner:

- Checks your cell phones, e-mails, or social networks without permission
- Exhibits extreme jealousy or insecurity

- Constantly belittles you or puts you down
- Displays an explosive temper
- Isolates you from family and friends
- Makes false accusations
- Demonstrates erratic mood swings
- Physically inflicts pain or hurts you in any way
- Acts possessive of you
- Tells you what to do, what to wear, where you can go, or who you can see
- Repeatedly pressures you to have sex

Anyone Can Be a Victim

Even though young women between the ages of sixteen and twenty-four experience the highest rate of dating violence—almost triple the national average—both men and women can be victims of abuse by their partners. The ways men and women abuse each other differ. Girls are more likely to yell, threaten to hurt themselves, pinch, slap, scratch, or kick their male partners. Young men more frequently engage in emotional, physical, and sexual abuse. Lesbian, gay, bisexual, and transgender teens are not exempt from dating violence. A 2013 study of LGBT teens showed significantly higher rates for an LGBT youth to be either a victim of dating violence or abusive toward his or her partner as compared to heterosexual teens.

CHAPTER 2

Why Does Dating Violence Happen?

Lauren Astley knew her ex-boyfriend, Nathaniel Fujita, was having a hard time getting over their breakup. Fujita didn't want their three-year relationship to end. But with help from her parents,

Lauren Astley

Mom&Dad-I can't really put into words how much I appreciate everything you did/do for me, but thanks. Love you.

*$-you girls are incredible, lets stay friends forever ok?
nf-thanks for everything

WE MADE IT 2011, HAVE FUN OUT THERE!

During her senior year of high school Lauren Astley was murdered by her ex-boyfriend, Nate Fujita. Lauren's family established the Lauren Dunne Astley Memorial Fund to raise awareness of dating violence and to promote healthy teen relationships.

Lauren broke it off for good a few weeks before they both graduated from their Wayland, Massachusetts, high school. However, when Nate withdrew from his friends, Lauren began to worry about him. Known for being a caring and loyal friend, Lauren reached out to Nate via text message. After weeks of avoiding her messages, Nate finally agreed to meet with his ex-girlfriend. The next day, Lauren's body was found in a nature preserve five miles (eight kilometers) from Nate's home. Nate had strangled Lauren, stabbed her multiple times, and slashed her throat. Nate was convicted of first-degree murder and sentenced to life in prison.

Dating Violence Is About Power and Control

Dating violence is about power and control over another person. Dating abuse can happen to anyone, regardless of age, gender, ethnicity, sexual orientation, education level, or income. It can occur on a first date or years into a relationship. For Fujita and many other abusers, dating violence also occurs when abusers don't know how to constructively handle feelings of anger and disappointment.

Teens often learn how to behave in relationships by watching their peers, the adults in their lives, or messages they receive from the media. Too often these examples can suggest that violence in a relationship—whether it's physical, emotional, or sexual abuse— is acceptable or even normal. Understanding the causes of dating violence can help you recognize warning signs that you or a friend may be involved with a person who could become violent in a relationship.

Violent behavior often stems from a person's inability to manage uncomfortable or complex emotions, such as anger,

MYTHS and *FACTS*
ABOUT DATING VIOLENCE

MYTH   If their partner hits them, most people will end a relationship.

FACT   **Nearly 80 percent of women who have been physically abused continue to date their partners.**

Joi Partain established Empowered and Beautiful, an organization to help fellow survivors of dating violence. Partain was beaten with a pair of golf clubs by an ex-boyfriend. The assault resulted in twenty-two broken bones, and she now wears an eye patch.

MYTH Witnessing abuse as a child has no effect on whether a person will become an abuser.

 Men who have witnessed violence in their homes (e.g., violence between their parents or if their parents abused their children) are three times more likely to abuse their own wives and children.

MYTH Dating violence happens most often among those who are poor or in minority populations.

 Dating violence and relationship abuse can happen regardless of income, race, class, ethnicity, sexual orientation, gender, or intelligence.

frustration, and jealousy. Your family, community, and social settings influence how you learn to deal with relationship challenges, manage stress, and cope with emotionally charged situations. If your partner grew up in a violent home, was a victim of domestic abuse, or witnessed violence in his or her neighborhood, the chances are greater that he or she has learned to use violence as a way to cope with complicated emotions or to resolve problems.

Violent behavior doesn't come out of nowhere. Often, there are risk factors that increase the chances that people will use violence in their relationships.

A risk factor is defined as a trait or characteristic that can increase the likelihood of a person developing a disease or behaving in a certain way. Exposure to behavioral patterns is also a risk factor. In the same way that unsafe sex, high blood pressure, or tobacco and alcohol use can increase your chances of developing a serious health issue, exposure to domestic abuse, being a victim of abuse, or regularly witnessing violence in your community can increase the chances that you or your partner will use violence as a way to cope with emotions or to manage relationships. While risk factors do not cause violent behavior, they can contribute to how a person chooses to handle interpersonal obstacles. (That said, it is important to note that there are indeed many people who suffer at the hands of others and resolve never to initiate such negative behaviors themselves.)

According to recent research, a link exists between bullying and dating violence. Students who are not involved in bullying are significantly less likely to experience physical dating violence compared to students who are bullies or victims of bullying.

There are four sets of risk factors—individual, family, peer/social, and community—that can increase the likelihood that your partner will be violent in a relationship.

Individual risk factors are the biological, psychological, and emotional characteristics we all possess that can influence our behaviors. Many violent people have been shown to have similar individual risk factors that contribute to aggressive or violent actions. These factors can include:

- Being a victim of abuse
- Attention deficits, hyperactivity, or learning disorders
- A history of aggressive behavior as a child
- Drug, alcohol, or tobacco use
- Low IQ
- Inability to control behavior
- History of emotional problems
- Exposure to violence in the family

Family risk factors are those that involve family life, such as how one was raised, and how the parents, caretakers, or guardians behaved (and continue to behave) at home. Family risk factors can include:

- Strict or severe parenting
- Harsh, lax, or inconsistent forms of discipline
- Low or no parental involvement
- Low or no emotional attachment to parents or parental figures
- Limited parental education and income
- Drug and alcohol abuse by parents
- Poor family functioning
- Poor supervision of children by parents

DATING VIOLENCE IS TOO COMMON

According to the 2013 Intimate Partner Violence in the United States survey, conducted by the U.S. Department of Justice's Bureau of Justice and Statistics, young women between the ages of sixteen and twenty-four experience the highest rates of intimate partner violence, almost triple the national average. Below are some of the most current statistics about dating violence:

- In a single year, almost 1.5 million high school students in the United States experience some form of physical abuse by the person with whom they are romantically involved.
- One out of every three adolescents in the United States is a victim of physical, sexual, emotional, or verbal abuse from a dating partner.
- One in ten high school students has been purposefully hit, slapped, or physically hurt by his or her partner.
- One quarter of all high school girls have been victims of physical or sexual abuse.
- Roughly 70 percent of all college students, male and female, report being sexually coerced by a romantic partner.
- Teens say confusion about what constitutes dating violence, misunderstanding of laws, and a desire to keep their abuse confidential are the top barriers to reporting it.
- Eighty-one percent of parents believe that dating violence is not an issue.

Peer and social risk factors are those that come from relationships with friends or peer groups. In peer groups that are violent, there is often pressure to act in certain ways or conform to how the group acts. If a group uses violence, it may be expected that everyone in the group use violence, too. Some examples of peer and social risk factors are:

- Hanging out with delinquent or violent peers
- Gang involvement or membership
- Social rejection by peers or a peer group
- Lack of involvement in school or formally organized activities
- Poor academic performance
- Low commitment or little interest in school

A community is a group of people living in the same place who share common characteristics. Community risk factors are those that affect the majority of people living in the same area or neighborhood. Examples of community risk factors that can influence violent behavior include:

- Limited economic opportunities
- Large populations of poor residents
- Repeated family disruptions
- Little communal interest in community participation

Causes of Dating Violence

While risk factors can influence how a person handles the ups and downs of a relationship, dating violence can be caused by other factors, such as low self-esteem, inexperience, upbringing, peer pressure, and immaturity.

Low self-esteem: Self-esteem is defined as how you value your-self. If your partner has low self-esteem, he or she may try to control your behavior because he or she may not feel worthy of your affection or interest. If you have low self-esteem, you may not believe that you deserve to be treated with respect, that you deserve the affections of someone popular or good looking, or that you are worthy of being loved.

Inexperience: As a teenager, you are beginning to learn how relationships work, how to treat one another, and how to handle the complex feelings you begin to have when you start dating. Domestic violence support groups recognize that dating violence is often accepted by teens as a normal part of a relationship because teens have little or no comparative dating experience. You may not realize that being teased inappropriately, being called hurtful names, being pressured to engage in sexual activities you aren't ready for, or that being hit or slapped amounts to dating violence.

Children who grow up with parents who engage in physical discipline and verbal abuse may well repeat these behaviors in their own relationships. Others, knowing the pain firsthand, steer clear of emulating such actions.

Upbringing: Not all parents share the same views when it comes to raising children. Some parents believe hitting children and being verbally abusive are acceptable forms of discipline. If you witness your parents being abusive toward one another or toward you and your siblings, you may believe that this is normal family behavior. Teens often repeat behaviors they see their parents exhibit. If you or your partner is abused at home, you are more likely to be abused or become involved with an abuser.

Peer pressure: As a teen, you are still learning how to interact in a variety of different social settings. You may want to be accepted by a peer group and may feel pressured to present a certain image to that group of friends. If you hang out with friends who use violence in their relationships, you may feel as though you have to show that you, too, can control your partner through abuse or violence.

Immaturity: Romantic relationships, even ones involving young adults, can be complicated and difficult. You may feel as though you're old enough to date, but you may still be experiencing a wide range of immature emotions. These emotions can then make you feel ill equipped to handle the more mature aspects of a relationship. This immaturity can lead you to respond to issues in your relationship by becoming jealous, wanting to control the other person, or by hitting or slapping your partner. Instead of telling your partner how you feel and expressing your emotions, you find yourself calling him or her names or punishing your partner by withholding affection.

CHAPTER 3

Coping with Dating Violence

Rae Anne Spence liked everything about her classmate Marcus McTear. "He was very, very sweet to me. We talked to like 3 o'clock in the morning every school night," Rae Anne told ABC's *20/20* for a special report on dating violence. Marcus, a running back on the football team at Reagan High School in Austin, Texas, showered Rae Anne with flowers, love notes, and constant affection. Before long, however, Marcus changed. He began telling Rae Anne what to do and what she was allowed to wear. He even began demanding that she not attract other boys' attention. "I couldn't show a lot of skin," Rae Anne said. "And with the makeup, if I would wear it, like, even a little bit, he would get mad."

It was Rae Anne's mother who noticed the change in her daughter's behavior. Her once bubbly, outgoing daughter was becoming withdrawn and less confident. When Marcus pushed Spence down the stairs at school, Rae Anne told her mother about his behavior, and her mother tried to persuade her daughter to end the relationship. The violence escalated until Marcus hit Rae Anne violently with a notebook during class. Rae Anne slapped him back in defense. But Marcus only grew angrier. He put Rae Anne in a headlock and began punching her until a teacher could intervene.

Rae Anne's mother had had enough. She moved the family across town to a different school district to get her daughter away

November is Dating Violence Awareness and Prevention Month. Organizations around the country offer events to honor abuse victims and encourage an open dialogue on dating violence, repairing or severing relationships as warranted, and having new relationships begin with recognition and respect.

from Marcus. It was a decision that might have saved her daughter's life. Marcus quickly moved on and found a new girlfriend, a sophomore named Ortralla Mosley. Less than nine months later, Marcus murdered Ortralla in a second-floor hallway of the school. He is now in prison serving a forty-year sentence.

Reactions to Dating Violence

It could be viewed by some as an extreme decision for Rae Anne Spence's mother to move her family away from her daughter's violent boyfriend. But Rae Anne's mother saw the effect, firsthand, of how Marcus McTear's abuse was negatively influencing her daughter. From worrying about every piece of clothing she wore to making the conscious decision to stop wearing makeup to avoid angering Marcus, Rae Anne was living in fear of what her boyfriend might do.

Like Rae Anne, many teens react to dating violence in a range of ways. Some think it's their fault or that they instigated the abuse. Many feel angry, sad, lonely, depressed, or confused by what's happening to them. Others feel threatened, humiliated by the abuse, or helpless to stop it from happening.

Abusers often create an environment in which victims always feeling uncertain as to what might happen next. Abusers act erratically: obsessively in love with you one day, physically or verbally assaulting you the next. They also try to isolate you so you feel as though there is nowhere to go and no one to trust. The roller coaster of abuse followed by intense affection followed again by abuse can play havoc with your emotions. You might feel as though you can't or shouldn't talk to family and friends about what's happening in your relationship. If you do tell someone, you might feel protective of your partner or defend his or her actions when peers or adults try to intervene in an attempt to end the relationship. You might also fear what will happen if your abuser finds out you told someone about what was happening.

The effects of dating violence don't end when the latest round of abuse stops. Instead, they can be felt throughout the relationship, even during times when your partner is peaceful or loving toward you. In addition to the physical injuries inflicted by your abuser—ranging from cuts, bruises, and broken bones to internal injuries depending on how severe the abuse is—your body will react to stress and fear in a variety of ways. You can experience physical reactions to abuse, which can include difficulty breathing, anxiety attacks, high blood

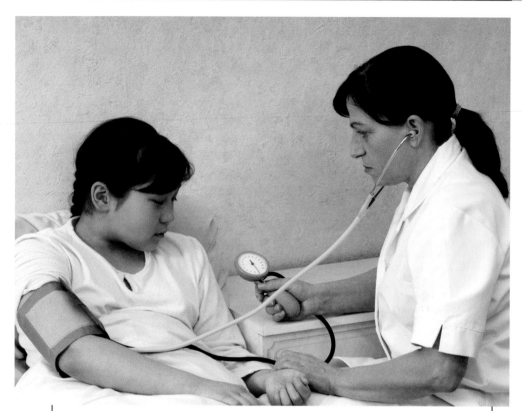

The effects of dating violence can extend well after the physical violence ends. Victims can experience physical reactions to the stress, fear, and uncertainty associated with abuse—including high blood pressure and anxiety.

pressure, and an increased heart rate. Your muscles may tighten as a result of the tension you feel from living in a heightened state of fear or uncertainty. You could experience sleeplessness, headaches, an increased or decreased appetite, or digestive problems from end-less worry. Abuse can cause you to suffer from acute stress disorder, which develops shortly after experiencing a traumatic event and can include severe anxiety, disassociation or detachment, or a decrease in emotional responsiveness.

Emotionally, you may experience shock or numbness, even denial or disbelief that someone would abuse you in this way.

You may feel angry about being abused and in a helpless situation. You might feel ashamed at allowing yourself to be abused or for staying with someone who abuses you.

Sometimes you may experience what are called secondary injuries. These injuries are those that are neither physical nor emotional, yet are hurtful because they cause their own degree of stress. A lack of understanding from friends or family, or their judgment of your actions, can be upsetting. They may comment on your choice of friend groups, especially if your friends are considered to be the "wrong crowd," or they may judge the clothing you wear or your actions as a way of suggesting that you could be to blame for the abuse you have suffered—a "blame the victim" response. These comments and judgments can all be insulting and painful to you. If you decide to press charges against your abuser, the stress of telling your story to law enforcement officials, being questioned by police, going through physical examinations to document injuries, and/or the mental anguish of having to face your abuser in court can contribute to secondary injuries.

WAYS TO PREVENT DATING VIOLENCE

No one deserves to be abused. While dating violence can be unexpected, there are things you can do to prevent it from happening and to keep yourself safe when you are out with someone new or someone you don't know very well.

Speaking to a therapist, a teacher, a trusted adult, or a licensed mental health professional can help you recognize signs of abuse, provide you with an outlet to recount your experiences in a safe environment, and teach you ways to protect yourself in the future.

Communicate your concerns: It can be difficult to ascertain if abuse is happening in your relationship. Unlike physical violence, emotional abuse can sometime be elusive and hard to pinpoint. If you're unsure about an incident or a comment your partner has made, talk to someone about it. Call a local or national dating or domestic violence hotline to speak to a professional about your relationship. If you'd rather talk to someone you know, seek out a trusted adult, such as a parent, a friend's parent, a teacher, a coach, a guidance counselor, or your religious leader.

(continued on the next page)

(continued from the previous page)

Educate yourself: Learn the signs of dating violence to find out what controlling behavior looks like and to understand what emotional abuse and demeaning comments sound like so you know when to seek help.

Date in groups: Some dating violence can happen as early as the first date. Physical violence is less likely to happen if you and your partner are with others. By dating with a group you can avoid being alone with someone you don't know well and have friends with you should something happen.

Avoid alcohol and drugs: Your inhibitions are lowered when you drink or take drugs. You can lose control of your decision-making abilities and become confused by your surroundings when you are impaired. Avoid drugs, don't accept an open container of alcohol from someone you don't know, and be aware of what and how much you are consuming to avoid being taken advantage of.

Be prepared: Situations can change unexpectedly. If you suddenly feel uncomfortable on a date, be prepared to leave. Always carry extra money and a cell phone with you. If you're prepared, you can call a friend for a ride or pay for a cab to get home safely.

Know the signs: Some behaviors, such as destroying your belongings or unpredictable mood swings, can be an indicator of future abuse. If you know the early warning signs of abuse, you can protect yourself.

Coping with Abuse

It can be hard to cope with the trauma of dating abuse. You may not know how to handle the complex feelings you are having, and you may find yourself experiencing an unhealthy response to the abuse you have suffered. Because you are emotionally involved with your partner and could have deep feelings for him or her, it's common to want to protect that person, make excuses for your partner's behavior, or lie to friends and family about what has occurred. Denial may even prevent you from acknowledging that abuse has occurred. To physically escape the situation, you may want to run away from home, or you may begin to think about attempting suicide. To escape emotionally or psychologically, you may begin using drugs, abusing alcohol, or caring less about school and your academics. You can experience a heightened sense of defensiveness and self-protection, which can lead to aggressive behavior or fighting with others. You may become more sexually active if you were sexually abused.

While these responses may be normal when suffering abuse, they are all dangerous, unhealthy ways to cope with being the victim of dating violence. To begin facing and healing from the abuse you've experienced, it's important to get away from your abuser to a safe place as soon as you can. Seek out a trusted adult with whom to speak and find a safe place to stay where you will be supported and protected from your partner. Once you are safe and secure, you can start to think about coping with the distress you've experienced. Emotionally you will be better able to make decisions about reporting the abuse to local authorities, seeking legal interventions, or getting counseling if you are in a calm, safe, and stable environment.

CHAPTER 4

Legal Protections and Rights

Dayna Marie Fure was a senior at Stanwood High School near Everett, Washington, and had plans to study law at Gonzaga University. The smart, athletic teen spent her eighteenth birthday in court getting an order of protection against her ex-boyfriend, twenty-three-year-old Mario Valentin. Fure and Valentin had dated for two years before she broke off the relationship. Immediately following the breakup, Valentin began harassing Fure. He confronted his ex-girlfriend at a nail salon where he pulled out a gun and told her was going to kill himself. The same night he showed up at her place of work, where he forced himself into her car, brandished the weapon again, and made more threats. Fure obtained a protective order to keep Valentin away from her, but friends and family reported later that they had seen Valentin violate the order several times. Within days of getting the protective order, Valentin shot and killed Fure before turning the gun on himself and committing suicide.

Fure's parents sued the Stanwood Police Department for failing to protect their daughter. The suit, which the family won, said the department downplayed or ignored the threat Valentin posed to Fure, failed to investigate reports of his violation of the protective

Clare's Law, established in Scotland in 2014, allows women to learn if their boyfriends have a history of abusive behavior. The law was created by Michael Brown, whose daughter Clare was murdered by her boyfriend. Clare did not know her boyfriend had a history of violence.

order, and, in some instances, did not attempt to locate Valentin for questioning after he made threats—*armed* threats—to Fure. Despite the number of such hostilities made to Fure, Valentin was never arrested or charged with a crime. It was later discovered that the department did not report some of his threats until *after* Fure was murdered.

You Have a Right to Feel Safe

The Stanwood Police Department's failure to protect Fure could have made the difference between life and death for the young woman. Increasingly, national domestic violence and dating abuse organizations—including Break the Cycle and the National Coalition Against Domestic Violence—are pressuring state and local law enforcement agencies to step up how they handle dating violence and relationship abuse experienced by teens. They are also at the forefront of advocating increased protections for minors who find themselves in violent or threatening relationships.

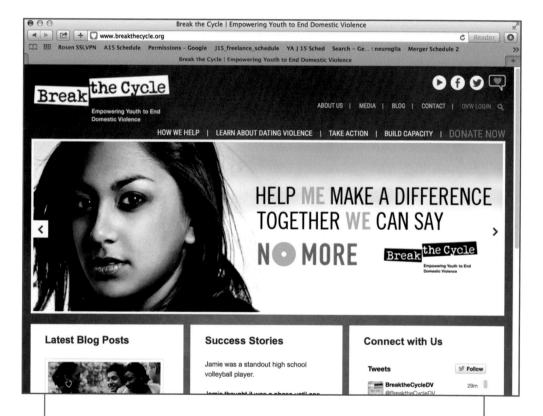

Break the Cycle (www.breakthecycle.org) offers advice, support, and education for teens to end the pattern of dating violence and domestic violence.

Due to these efforts, state and federal law enforcement agencies are beginning to better recognize the special circumstances that surround teen dating violence. However, all states define dating violence differently, and as a result, not all states provide the same protections to minors, which is the term the legal system and law enforcement agencies use when referring to people under the age of eighteen.

Some states explicitly allow minors to petition on their own behalf for a protective order. Other states prohibit minors from obtaining a protective order without parental involvement. Still others prohibit protective orders to be filed against abusers if the abuser is a minor. Three states offer protections to individuals in opposite-sex relationships but not to those in same-sex relationships. Essentially, the law varies for minors depending on the state. Because each state provides different levels of protection—or in some cases, no protection—for minors who are seeking legal intervention for dating violence, it's important to learn where your state stands. Some states allow minors to file for protective assistance without parental involvement. Others require parents to be involved right away to provide permission for their child to use services. In other states, the laws are vague, leaving it open to individual judges to contact a minor's parents if the judge thinks doing so is in the minor's best interest. A few states still restrict access to legal protections for minors in dating relationships, limiting the services and options available to young people who are being abused by their partners.

Some states have made dating-violence education mandatory in middle and high school, offering an opportunity for young men and women to understand what constitutes dating abuse, the various types that exist, and the early warning signs of violent behavior.

STATE LAW REPORT CARDS

How does your state stack up against others when it comes to providing you with protections against dating violence? Break the Cycle created the State Law Report Card to present an assessment of the protection orders of all fifty states and the District of Columbia. States with higher grades are more responsive to the needs of teens seeking protections and provide better services than states with lower grades.

Alabama	F	Kentucky	F	North Dakota	D
Alaska	B	Louisiana	C	Ohio	F
Arizona	B	Maine	B	Oklahoma	A
Arkansas	C	Maryland	C	Oregon	D
California	A	Massachusetts	B	Pennsylvania	D
Colorado	C	Michigan	C	Rhode Island	A
Connecticut	C	Minnesota	B	South Carolina	F
Delaware	B	Mississippi	B	South Dakota	F
District of Columbia	A	Missouri	F	Tennessee	B
Florida	B	Montana	C	Texas	C
Georgia	F	Nebraska	C	Utah	F
Hawaii	C	Nevada	C	Vermont	B
Idaho	C	New Hampshire	A	Virginia	F
Illinois	A	New Jersey	B	Washington	A
Indiana	B	New Mexico	B	West Virginia	B
Iowa	C	New York	B	Wisconsin	D
Kansas	C	North Carolina	C	Wyoming	C

Who Can You Turn To?

If you are being abused by your partner and decide that you need help from law enforcement officials, there are several people you can approach for the information you need in order to make a smart, informed decision.

Legal service providers: Legal service providers are trained professionals who can discuss all of the options available to you under your state's laws. They can help you create a safety plan tailored to your specific situation and can connect you to your local civil or criminal justice system.

Victim's advocates: These professionals are trained to support victims of crimes. Advocates provide information, offer emotional support, and help victims finding resources. They can also assist in explaining and helping you complete any legal paperwork. Sometimes, advocates go to court with victims. Advocates may also contact organizations, such as criminal justice or social service agencies, to get help or information for victims. Victim's advocates work in a variety of places, including police stations, nonprofit community organizations, and prosecutor's offices.

VICTIM'S RIGHTS

You have the right to feel safe in your relationships. You also have the right to be treated with respect and dignity if you file a complaint or press charges against your partner for domestic abuse or assault. You have rights as a victim of a crime. Victim's rights are laws that exist at the federal level in all fifty states requiring law enforcement to

(continued on the next page)

(continued from the previous page)

provide you with certain information about the legal system and the options and protections available to you that are enforced by local authorities. It also ensures that you have a role in the criminal justice process. Basic victim rights include:

- The right to be treated with dignity, respect, and sensitivity
- The right to be informed of rights, court and legal proceedings related to your case, and proceedings and court decisions related to your abuser
- The right to protection

Protective Orders

A powerful tool to help you leave an abusive relationship is a protection order. Sometimes called a restraining order, protection-from-abuse order, or peace order, a protective order is a judicial decree or ruling that restricts a person's movements and activities toward another person. It can protect you from coming into contact with your abuser and prevents the abuser from stalking, harassing, or communicating with you in any form. Your abuser cannot visit your house, call or text you, e-mail you, or otherwise harass you without facing a criminal penalty such as arrest or serving time in jail.

Protective orders can become difficult to enforce when both the victim and the abuser attend the same high school or college. In many states, school systems may not be responsible for

The National Domestic Violence
HOTLINE
1.800.799.SAFE (7233) • 1.800.787.3224 (TTY)

The National Domestic Violence Hotline connects you to advocates who can help you understand dating and domestic violence, providing you with lifesaving tools such as safety planning. There is also information on the organization's website, http://www.thehotline.org.

enforcing restraining orders under state law, though some will try to work with the victim to provide a measure of safety. If the protective order prevents the victim and the abuser from being in the same building, the school district may make a scheduling change to keep both students separate but ensure that both can continue to attend classes. Some school districts might offer home tutoring to one or both of the students involved.

CHAPTER 5

Getting Help

The Florida Coalition Against Domestic Violence (FCADV) has this story on its website as a representative example of domestic violence: Ashley started dating Benny when both of them were sophomores in high school. At first, Benny was nice to Ashley, always inviting her over to his house after school. The abuse started when Ashley would leave to go home. Benny would tell Ashley that she didn't care about him and that if she left there would be other girls who would want to stay and hang out with him.

After a few months, Benny began to isolate Ashley from her friends. He became possessive and jealous and would make fun of anyone Ashley hung around with. He'd also make Ashley feel guilty for spending time with her friends. He started to tell her what to wear to school and to whom she could talk. One afternoon Benny forced Ashley to have sex with him. Even though she told him she didn't want to and was afraid of getting pregnant, Benny slapped her and told her he would decide if she got pregnant or not.

Benny began stalking Ashley at school. He'd wait for her outside her classes and whisper threats in her ear. He'd send her text messages saying he knew where she was and what she was doing. One afternoon a teacher noticed Benny being rough with Ashley in the hallway after class. When Benny left, the teacher asked Ashley to come back into class to talk. The teacher told Ashley that she deserved to be treated better.

Being the victim of dating violence can make you feel helpless, but you aren't. You can seek help, learn how to end a violent relationship, and move on in a healthy, productive, and positive way.

Two weeks later, Ashley approached the teacher again and asked for help. With support from her teacher and her mother, Ashley broke up with Benny and changed schools. Ashley got the help she needed to end her relationship with Benny and begin to move on with her life.

Why People Stay in Violent Relationships

People stay in unhealthy or violent relationships for a variety of reasons. For many, it's the conflicting emotions that keep them tied to their abusers. Despite being abused, you may feel love and affection toward your partner. You may be afraid of what your abuser will do to you or your family if you leave, or you may believe abuse is normal if you grew up in a violent home or witnessed abusive relationships. There is also social pressure to stay. Your friends may not understand why you are breaking up with your partner, or you may be scared everyone will take his or her side.

It's important to remember that abuse of any kind does not have a role in a healthy, loving relationship and that no matter what your abuser says, it's never your fault. Nothing you say, do, or wear gives your partner the right to be violent toward you.

Seek Help

If you think that you are in an abusive relationship, get help immediately. Don't keep the abuse a secret. Seek out a trusted adult and tell him or her what you have been experiencing. If you choose to tell your story, you should know that some adults are mandatory reporters of abuse, meaning that they are legally required to report the abuse to a local law enforcement or child protective services agency. Teachers, counselors, social workers, therapists, and medical staff such as nurses and doctors are all mandatory reporters of domestic, child, and dating abuse and violence. That means that even if they wanted to keep your secret quiet, by law they cannot. This fact shouldn't discourage you from talking to someone. Local law enforcement may be able to step in and provide some much-needed protection for you, and you will be able to learn where else you can turn for help, support, or other services.

Decisions to Consider

Whether you report dating violence to the authorities or decide to keep the experience quiet, you may need to seek care for your injuries. You should never let injuries go untreated if someone has physically assaulted you. You could have internal injuries that could go unnoticed by you and become very serious without medical treatment. You also may need to be tested for pregnancy or sexually transmitted diseases, both of which require medical care. In addition to physical or sexual assault or injury, you may need counseling to help you cope with the complex and conflicting emotions you may be feeling. Counseling can help you sort out and understand your feelings, as well as help you regain a sense of control over your life.

Counselors are available at different places. You can get a referral by a doctor to speak with a counselor, or you may want to call an abuse hotline. These hotlines are free, confidential, and staffed with professionals who can provide advice and other services to you based on your individual situation.

Should you decide to report the abuse to law enforcement, you may want to talk to a victim's advocate to help you make this

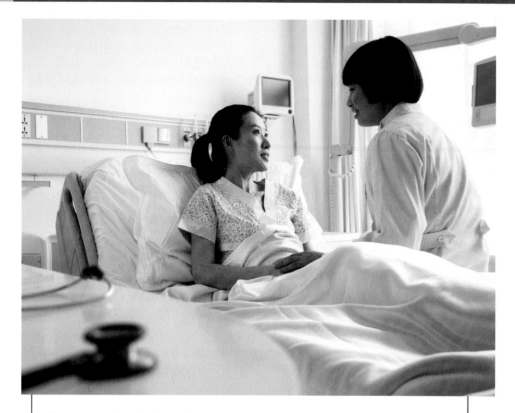

If you are the victim of physical violence, it's important to see a doctor. What might appear as minor injuries could in fact lead to major health issues. Some injuries or medical conditions—such as internal bleeding or a sexually transmitted disease—may require immediate medical care.

decision. A victim's advocate can guide you through the criminal justice system, assist you in filing the necessary paperwork, and help you solve problems that may arise.

Help Yourself

If you find yourself in a violent relationship but are reluctant to leave immediately, there are ways you can help yourself become safer until the time comes for you to escape the situation entirely. Begin to take precautions when you go out. Let your friends or family members know where you will be, when you expect to arrive at your destination, and when you expect to return home. Memorize important phone numbers and always keep money on hand to pay for a taxi, bus fare, or a subway ride so that you can get someplace safe. Keep a cell phone with you at all times.

When you go out, stay close to your group of friends, or go out with other couples. If you find yourself in an emergency situation, do not be afraid to call 911.

Moving On

It can be stressful and emotional to leave a relationship under healthy circumstances. When there has been a history of violence, it's even more important to get the help you need to move on and cope with the experiences you've had. Here are some tips:

- Reconnect with friends from whom you've drifted during the relationship. Tell them how you feel and what you've been going through. When you feel overwhelmed or panicked, call one of them to talk.
- Allow yourself to feel the pain of the breakup and to grieve the loss of your relationship.
- Spend time with your family and friends, but also by yourself so you can have the chance to sort out your feelings and understand who you are now.
- Take care of your mind and body. Get regular sleep and eat balanced, healthy meals. Get some exercise and find ways to manage any stress you may be feeling.
- Reestablish a normal routine as soon as possible. Go back to school, attend extracurricular activities, and if you have a job, return to work.

Moving on from an abusive relationship can be difficult. But if you surround yourself with caring family and friends and take the time you need to heal, you can cope with your experiences and proceed in a positive way. Many people find that yoga, meditation, and taking long walks provide restorative "me" time.

- Make daily decisions for yourself. By making decisions, even small ones, you can begin to bring back a feeling of control over your life and gain confidence in your ability to make choices and decisions.
- Be aware and attentive as you proceed with daily tasks. After experiencing severe stress, accidents are more likely to happen.
- Spend a few moments each day focusing on the things for which you are thankful, such as your friends and family, your talents and accomplishments, and the hopes and dreams you have for your future.

10 GREAT QUESTIONS TO ASK WHEN YOU'RE ASKING FOR HELP

1. If I ask for help, will my partner find out?

2. How do I end a relationship safely?

3. Where can I go to feel safe?

4. What will happen if I report the abuse to law enforcement?

5. Do I have to tell my parents about the abuse?

6. How can I be in love with someone who hurts me?

7. How can someone who loves me abuse me?

8. What if no one believes me about the abuse?

9. How can I help a friend whom I know is being abused?

10. Can I get my partner help?

Help a Friend

If you know someone who is in a violent relationship or you witness someone being abused by his or her partner, you can offer
support and encourage him or her to seek help. Express your
concerns for the victim's well-being. If that person chooses to
talk to you about the relationship in question, be a good listener.
Resist the urge to say what to do or pressure him or her to end
the relationship. Instead, encourage your friend to speak to an
adult or call a dating violence or domestic abuse hotline. Offer
your support and friendship, and ask how you can help. If your

Help a friend who may be experiencing dating violence by
staying supportive, encouraging her to talk to a professional,
and continuing to offer your friendship.

friend decides to stay with his or her partner, don't be judgmental. Knowing when to leave or seek help is a personal decision. As your friend makes decisions about his or her relationship, remain supportive and loyal. Avoid the temptation to confront your friend's abuser about the abuse. This approach can be dangerous for both you and your friend.

You Can Break Free and Move On

You may never expect to find yourself in a violent relationship, but if you do, there are resources available to help you end it and provide you with some safety as your rebuild your life. Don't be afraid to ask for help. The effects of an unhealthy relationship can last a lifetime. By educating yourself and your friends about dating violence, knowing the warning signs of violent and controlling behavior, and being aware of the places and people to whom you can turn, you can begin to free yourself from a world of hurt and open yourself up to the joy, freedom, and love of life that each of us deserves.

GLOSSARY

ASCERTAIN To learn or find out something, such as information or the truth.

COERCION The act or process of achieving a result using force or threats.

CRITICISM The act of expressing disapproval and of noting the problems or faults of a person or thing.

DECREE An official decision made by a court of law.

DELINQUENT A young person who regularly does illegal or immoral things.

ETHNICITY A particular affiliation or group sharing the same race, religion, linguistic, or cultural background.

FIRST-DEGREE MURDER An unlawful killing that is both willful and premeditated or planned.

HETEROSEXUAL Someone who is sexually attracted to people of the opposite sex.

HUMILIATION Reducing or lowering of a position in one's own eyes or others' eyes, causing the object of such treatment to feel foolish or ashamed.

INTERPERSONAL Being, relating to, or involving relations between and among people.

INTERVENTION The act or process of becoming involved in something (such as a conflict) in order to have an influence on what happens.

INTIMIDATION The act of compelling someone to behave in a certain way by the use of fear or threats.

MANIPULATION Using controlling language or behavior to affect the will of another so that he or she responds to one's own advantage.

POSSESSIVENESS Wanting all of someone's attention and love.

SEXUAL ORIENTATION An enduring pattern of romantic or sexual attraction (or a combination of these) to members of the opposite sex or gender, the same sex or gender, or to both sexes or more than one gender. In other words, a way to describe whether one is heterosexual, homosexual, or bisexual.

TRANSGENDER Of or relating to people who have a sexual identity that differs from the sex they were at birth.

FOR MORE INFORMATION

Break the Cycle
P.O. Box 66165
Washington, DC 20035
(202) 824-0707
Website: http://www.breakthecycle.org
Break the Cycle is the leading national nonprofit organization
    working to provide comprehensive dating abuse prevention
    programs exclusively to young people. Whether it's
    innovating violence prevention programs, hosting public
    campaigns, or championing effective laws and policies, Break
    the Cycle inspires and supports young people in preventing
    and escaping unhealthy relationships.

DATE SAFE Project
P.O. Box 20906
Greenfield, WI 53220-0906
(920) 326-3687
Website: http://www.datesafeproject.org
The DATE SAFE Project provides positive how-to skills and
    helpful insights for addressing verbal consent, respecting of
    boundaries, sexual decision-making, bystander intervention,
    and supporting survivors.

Hardy Girls, Healthy Women
P.O. Box 821
Waterville, ME 04903-0821
(207) 861-8131
Website: http://www.hghw.org
Hardy Girls, Healthy Women is a nonprofit organization
    dedicated to the health and well-being of girls and women.

Its vision is that all girls and women experience equality, independence, and safety in their everyday lives.

Love Is Respect
Chat at www.loveisrespect.org
Text loveis to 22522*
(866) 331-9474
Website: http://www.loveisrespect.org/
Loveisrespect.org has highly trained peer advocates who offer support, information, and advocacy to young people who have questions or concerns about their dating relationships. The organization provides information and support not only to those people in troubling relationships, but also to concerned friends and family members, teachers, counselors, service providers, and members of law enforcement.

National Center on Domestic and Sexual Violence
(512) 407-9020
Website: http://www.ncdsv.org
The National Center on Domestic and Sexual Violence is an organization that has encouraged and created unprecedented levels of collaboration among professionals working to end violence against women.

National Domestic Violence Hotline
P.O. Box 161810
Austin, TX 78716
(800) 799-SAFE
Website: http://www.thehotline.org
Operating around the clock, seven days a week, confidential

and free of cost, the National Domestic Violence Hotline provides lifesaving tools and immediate support to enable victims to find safety and live lives free of abuse. The organization's website offers useful tools on defining abuse, information on where to go for help, and resources for both victims and abusers.

National Online Resource Center for Violence Against
    Women (VAWnet)
3605 Vartan Way, Suite 101
Harrisburg, PA 17110
(800) 537-2238
Website: http://www.vawnet.org
VAWnet is a comprehensive and easily accessible online
    collection of full-text searchable materials and resources on
    domestic violence, sexual violence, and related issues.

Websites

Because of the changing nature of Internet links, Rosen Publishing has developed an online list of websites related to the subject of this book. This site is updated regularly. Please use this link to access the list:

http://www.rosenlinks.com/CVAW/Date

Andrews, Arin. *Some Assembly Required: The Not-So-Secret Life of a Transgendered Teen.* New York, NY: Simon & Schuster Books for Young Readers, 2014.

Burningham, Sarah O'Leary, and Keri Smith. *Boyology: A Teen Girl's Crash Course in All Things Boy.* San Francisco, CA: Chronicle Books, 2012.

Eastham, Chad. *The Truth About Dating, Love & Just Being Friends.* Nashville, TN: Thomas Nelson/HarperCollins Christian Publishing, 2011.

Evans, Patricia. *Teen Torment: Overcoming Verbal Abuse at Home and at School.* Fort Collins, CO: Adams Media Corporation, 2003.

Evert, Jason. *If You Really Loved Me: 100 Questions on Dating, Relationships and Sexual Purity.* El Cajon, CA: Catholic Answers, 2009.

Fonda, Jane. *Being a Teen: Everything Teen Girls & Boys Should Know About Relationships, Sex, Love, Health, Identity & More.* New York, NY: Random House Trade Paperbacks, 2014.

Gerdes, Louise. *Teen Dating.* Independence, KY: Greenhaven Press, 2013.

Hunter, Joanna V. *But He'll Change: End the Thinking That Keeps You in an Abusive Relationship.* Center City, MN: Hazelden Publishing, 2010.

Lawton, Sandra Augustyn. *Abuse and Violence Information for Teens: Health Tips About the Causes and Consequences of Abusive and Violent Behavior.* Detroit, MI: Omnigraphics, Inc., 2007.

Levy, Barrie. *In Love and in Danger: A Teen's Guide to Breaking Free of Abusive Relationships.* Berkeley, CA: Seal Press, 2006.

Lily, Henrietta M. *Teen Mental Health: Dating Violence.* New York, NY: Rosen Publishing Group, 2011.

Murray, Jill A. *But He Never Hit Me: The Devastating Cost of Non-Physical Abuse to Girls and Women.* Bloomington, IN: iUniverse, 2007.

Sorenson McGee, Kathleen, and Laura Holmes Buddenberg. *Unmasking Sexual Con Games.* Boystown, NV: Boystown Press, 2003.

Waldal, Elin Stebbins. *Tornado Warning: A Memoir of Teen Dating Violence and Its Effect on a Women's Life.* Carlsbad, CA: Sound Beach Publishing, 2011.

ABC News. "Teen Shares Tragic Story of a Violent First Love."
    January 8, 2014. Retrieved October 16, 2014 (http://
    abcnews.go.com/GMA/story?id=125452&page=1&
    singlePage=true).

ABC News. "Tragic Tale of Teen Dating." November 10, 2006.
    Retrieved October 16, 2014 (http://abcnews.go.com/2020/
    Health/story?id=630874&page=1&singlePage=true).

Arnold, Kevin D. "How to Diagnose an Unhealthy Relationship."
    March 15, 2014. Retrieved October 14, 2014 (http://www
    .psychologytoday.com/blog/the-older-dad/201403/how
    -diagnose-unhealthy-relationship).

Break the Cycle. "Know Your Rights." Retrieved October 21,
    2014 (http://www.breakthecycle.org/know-your-rights).

Break the Cycle. "State Law Report Cards." Retrieved October
    21, 2014 (http://www.breakthecycle.org/state-law
    -report-cards).

Bureau of Justice Statistics. "Intimate Partner Violence:
    Attributes of Victimization, 1993–2011." November 2013.
    Retrieved October 16, 2014 (http://www.bjs.gov/content/
    pub/pdf/ipvav9311.pdf).

Dank, M., P. Lachman, J. M. Zweig, and J. Yahner. "Dating
    Violence Experiences of Lesbian, Gay, Bisexual, and
    Transgender Youth." *Journal of Youth and Adolescence*, 2013.

Domestic Violence Action Center. "What About Teen Dating
    Violence?" Retrieved October 20, 2014 (http://www
    .stoptheviolence.org/dv-teen-dating-violence).

Domestic Violence & Sexual Assault Services. "Myths and
    Facts: Dating Violence." Retrieved October 27, 2014 (http://
    www.dvsas.org/pages/Information-and-Resources/
    Domestic-Violence/Dating-Violence-Quiz).

Florida Coalition Against Domestic Violence. "Stories of
    Domestic Violence." Retrieved October 24, 2014 (http://
    www.fcadv.org/about/stories-of-domestic-violence).

Hewlett, Michael. "Forsyth Student's Restraining Order Against
    Another Student Raises Legal Questions." November 4,
    2012. Retrieved October 21, 2014 (http://www.journalnow
    .com/news/local/article_91c8597e-26fa-11e2-8cd9
    -0019bb30f31a.html).

Ireland, Kay. "Causes of Violence in Teen Dating." November
    21, 2013. Retrieved October 15, 2014 (http://www
    .livestrong.com/article/248483-causes-of-violence-in
    -teen-dating).

LiveStrong.com. "Ways to Prevent Dating Violence." January 3,
    2014. Retrieved October 20, 2014 (http://www.livestrong
    .com/article/143562-ways-prevent-dating-violence).

LoveIsRespect.org. "National Survey of Teen Dating Violence
    Laws." Retrieved October 21, 2014 (http://www
    .loveisrespect.org/get-help/legal-help/
    the-national-survey-of-teen-dating-violence-laws).

Martin, Jill, and Steve Almasy. "Ray Rice Terminated by Team,
    Suspended by NFL After New Violent Video." CNN,
    September 16, 2014. Retrieved October 6, 2014 (http://
    www.cnn.com/2014/09/08/us/ray-rice-new-video).

Office on Women's Health, U.S. Department of Health and
    Human Services. "Violence Against Women: Dating
    Violence." Retrieved October 14, 2014 (http://www
    .womenshealth.gov/violence-against-women/types-of
    -violence/dating-violence.html).

About the Author

Laura La Bella is the author of many nonfiction children's books. She has profiled actress and activist Angelina Jolie in *Celebrity Activists: Angelina Jolie, Goodwill Ambassador to the UN*; reported on the declining availability of the world's fresh water supply in *Not Enough to Drink: Pollution, Drought, and Tainted Water Supplies*; and examined the food industry in *Safety and the Food Supply*. La Bella earned a bachelor's degree in journalism and a master's degree in marketing. She lives in Rochester, New York, with her husband and sons.

Photo Credits

Cover © iStockphoto.com/Katarzyna Bialasiewicz; p. 5 Andrew Burton/Getty Images; p. 8 Fuse/Getty Images; p. 11 BernardaSv/iStock/Thinkstock; p. 13 Peter Bernik/Shutterstock.com; p. 16 Boston Globe/Getty Images; p. 18 Orlando Sentinel/McClatchy-Tribune/Getty Images; p. 20 Photofusion/Universal Images Group/Getty Images; p. 24 Monkey Business Images/Shutterstock.com; p. 27 © Leonard Ortiz/The Orange County Register/ZUMA Press; p. 29 Anette Romanenko/iStock/Thinkstock; p. 31 AlexRaths/iStock/Thinkstock; p. 35 Press Association/AP Images; p. 36 breakthecycle.org. Used with permission; p. 41 PR Newswire/AP Images; p. 43 © Chris Rout/Alamy; p. 46 XiXinXing/iStock/Thinkstock; p. 48 shironosov/iStock/Thinkstock; p. 50 antikainen/iStock/Thinkstock.

Designer: Nicole Russo; Executive Editor: Hope Lourie Killcoyne